This is BRISTOL

John Trelawny-Ross
& Bryan Little

REDCLIFFE
Bristol

First published in 1982 by
Redcliffe Press Ltd,
14 Dowry Square, Bristol 8

ISBN 0 905459 28 8

Designed by Nicholas Bassett

Printed in Great Britain by
Burleigh Ltd, Bristol

CONTENTS

ACKNOWLEDGEMENTS

The illustrations in this book are, in the main, the work of John Trelawny-Ross. However, the publishers acknowledge with thanks permission to reproduce the following:

British Aerospace and W.D. & H.O. Wills for the photographs of factory interiors; City of Bristol Museum and Art Gallery and John Harvey & Sons Ltd for the relevant photographs in the Museums and Artefacts section; Bristol Polytechnic for St. Matthias College; the University of Bristol for the photograph of Goldney Grotto and of Hiatt Baker Hall; Gordon Kelsey for the National Westminster Bank interior, the Royal Fort ceiling and the Malt & Hops interior; Brian Middlehurst for the photograph of The Lochiel; and the Port of Bristol Authority for the photographs of shipping at Avonmouth and Royal Portbury Docks.

An Introduction

From whatever direction, by rail or road, visitors come to Bristol one thing must immediately strike them. Bristol is very large: far larger than, say, Bath or Gloucester, Exeter or Worcester, much larger also than Cardiff, its nearest reasonable rival in size or population. Within its official boundaries it has some 390,000 people, but add such adjacent areas as Filton, Downend, Mangotsfield and Kingswood, and a small fringe on what was once the Somerset side of the city, and one finds that something like 600,000 people live in the urban expanse from Avonmouth to Brislington or from Warmley to the great hill of Dundry whose upper slopes are still, above the city boundary, a happily rural stretch of fields and hedges. Thanks to its southern green belt, and to the general economics of the West of England, Bristol is not part of a 'conurbation'. But it is easily the largest English city West of London or South of Birmingham.

Such a standing, among modern British cities, could only come from the city's role as a great centre of commerce, distribution, administration and industry. For these same reasons, whatever their origins and comparatively modest early history, such provincial cities as Birmingham, Liverpool, Manchester, Sheffield and Leeds are all large and wide-spreading – larger in fact and more 'conurbated' than Bristol but with past history and present appearance very different from that in the chief city of the new county of Avon.

An essential point becomes clear once our visitor reaches the original heart of Bristol on its neck of land between the Avon arm of the Floating Harbour and its largely concealed, much smaller tributary the Frome. A complex of narrow streets and lanes, with a rich variety of ancient and historic buildings – notably churches and the ruins of bombed churches – shows that central Bristol, like the City of London, is an ancient town with a long history of commercial prominence. Some of the suburbs, with fine houses of the eighteenth century, bring home the same point. From the city's layout, and from this wealth of historic architecture, much of it medieval, one soon sees that Bristol has been a place of great importance for many centuries, and for much longer than the two hundred years since the start of the Industrial Revolution. While the great northern and Midland cities have been in the front rank of extent and population only since the later decades of the eighteenth century, Bristol – in the Middle Ages and most notably in the first half of the Georgian period – has been among the front runners for over eight centuries. Commerce and industry are by no means the whole of the Bristol story. But they are the constant, deciding theme of a record which has, in the last one hundred years, developed notably in other directions. The port, the activities of merchants, traders and bankers, and manufacturing industry have been the main causes of the city's growth from a medieval population of less than 15,000, to the larger urban complex and vastly greater population of today.

Another striking point about Bristol is its natural scenery. Its two rivers, more notably the Avon, cut through rocky hill ridges which make veritable gorges of parts of their valleys, giving them an aspect far more dramatic than that of such tidal estuaries as the Mersey, the Humber, and the Thames. The scenery of much of Bristol is deeply and dramatically conditioned by these river approaches and by the hill ridges, modest in height but steep-sided and making, in many parts of the city, for stiff gradients and for skilfully sited houses, whose windows command enviably dramatic views over expanses of water or across the city. Many of these views also include rural stretches, on Dundry for instance and in the last ridge of the Cotswolds near Bath. Not being part of a conurbation Bristol is a city isolated from other large industrial towns. Real country is never far away, and no-one who wishes to work in Bristol and yet live in the country need travel for more than a dozen miles.

It has been said, of Clifton, that it is Britain's most beautiful suburb. Here, between the long highway of Pembroke Road and the edge of the Avon Gorge, romantic scenery and mainly Georgian architecture combine brilliantly to make a favoured district which adds vastly to the quality of the city which now contains it. In the area of Henbury and Kingsweston one has the strongly romantic setting of a deep, wooded gorge, the accompaniment of romantic and classical architecture with a superlative 'village picturesque' hamlet thrown in, which gives Bristol a parkland treasure which no visitor should miss, and which tourists from abroad find notably exciting.

The beauties of Clifton and the Blaise estate, added to the quality of the entertainment – musical, artistic, and theatrical – available in Bristol, have their bearing on a way of life more gracious than that often, though wrongly, associated with cities so commercial and industrial. Bristol, thanks in part to the Hotwells clientèle and, later, to the sort of people who made their homes in Clifton, has never been a cultural desert any more than the cities which harbour the Huddersfield Choral Society, the Hallé Orchestra, or the Birmingham Repertory Theatre. Bristol University's great growth in the last thirty years, and the presence in the city of many other places of higher education, have widened out the quality of Bristol's life, so that much of Clifton has now taken on the aspect, and liveliness, which one readily associates with a University city.

Bristol is also a city highly deserving of the appreciation of visitors from within this country and abroad. Many of them find that the city is worth much more than a fleeting, one-night break in a package tour which has also looked in on such provincial attractions as Oxford, the Wye Valley, and Stratford on its other Avon.

The notion of tourism leads one to compare Bristol with some much visited cities abroad. No close parallel exists between Bristol and, say, Antwerp, Venice or Florence, though one famous Bristol church tower invites comparison with the best known feature of Pisa. But for cities which are still 'touristic', with scenic attractions, abundant fine buildings and long histories of commercial eminence and cultural achievement one may, without straining resemblances and apart from Bristol's aptly chosen French partner city of Bordeaux, quote one city in the Low countries and one in northern Italy.

Bristol has been described, with a special reference to its Floating Harbour, as Britain's Amsterdam. The concentric *grachten* of Amsterdam are actually little like Bristol's Floating Harbour, and Bristol's buildings no longer include a wealth of seventeenth-century houses. But Amsterdam, with its harbour, industries not far away and the artistic glories of the Concertgebouw, its old buildings and its art galleries is still, on its larger scale, within the same category at Bristol. Then on the Ligurian coast, with a scenic background even more dramatic than Bristol's Avon Gorge, Italy's chief port of Genoa has for centuries had a busy harbour, industry and commerce blended with a live cultural history, ancient churches of various dates and styles and Renaissance *palazzi* which house University faculties or the offices of shipping and commercial concerns.

The first section of this book illustrates the scenery of Bristol and its approaches. We then show the complex of rivers and waterways combining to create the Floating Harbour which cuts through the central city, partly by way of natural rivers but on two occasions much modified by human planning and ingenuity and by the sweat and muscle of those who worked on the harbour as it has been since 1247 and 1809. Next comes a little on the present activity of the port, and of the commerce and industry which support over half a million people in Bristol and just outside it. The next views give some picturesque glimpses of Bristol's historic streetscape, mostly in or near the original centre, but reaching out as far as the great tower of the University and houses on St. Michael's Hill. Important separate buildings follow, among them some of Bristol's great variety of churches; so, too, do some of the city's numerous almshouses and a few of its picturesque and historic inns. The next section takes the reader to Hotwells and Clifton and to Henbury parish with its rich choice of scenic and monumental delights. A section on higher education follows, and we conclude with a look at the city's many museums and collections of applied art and craftsmanship, notably of the eighteenth century.

SCENERY

The many delights of Bristol's natural scenery come from the deep, steep-sided valleys of the city's two rivers and their tributary streams, from jealously guarded open spaces, and from woodlands whose extent and rich variety of trees are unusual in a large commercial and industrial town. Hill ridges, of no great height but often steeply sloping, also produce many attractive scenes and townscape effects.

The most famous, and the best loved of Bristol's scenic beauties, is the

Clifton Gorge, deeply cleft between the precipices of Clifton and Sea Walls and the less dramatic, but steeply tumbling and now well-wooded slopes of Leigh Woods on what was, until the reclassification of county boundaries in 1974, the Somerset side of the Bristol Avon. Even without the enhancement of the Suspension Bridge, which marked a triumph of man's ingenuity over the untamed wilds of romantic nature, the Gorge makes a splendid scene, the more remarkable in that one side of it is part of a great city of nearly half a million people. One may compare it, without detriment, to the point in the Rhine's deep-cut channel where on one side the Lorelei rock towers up over the busily navigated stream.

The gorge like valley of the Avon above the city, and the deep, well-wooded course of Bristol's smaller river, one of many Fromes in the western counties, also contribute, with distinction, to the city's scenery.

Running back from the riverside precipices of Clifton and Sea Walls the great sweep of Clifton and Durdham Downs, extending over more than 450 acres, gives Bristol an open space of rare quality. Yet despite their unsophisticated and 'natural' appearance the Downs are as much a man-made landscape as any park laid out by 'Capability' Brown or Humphrey Repton; they need, and receive, careful protection and replanting by a special committee charged with their maintenance. It is easy on the Downs, as can be seen from our view of trees, shrubs and grassland, to forget that the more urban scene of Bristol's residential suburbs is so near at hand. Sea air blows briskly in from the Severn's tidal estuary; it has been said that 'Dr. Downs is the best physician in Bristol'.

Most of Bristol's hill scenery comes in long ridges, some rising nearly 300 feet above sea level. But one hill, dramatically close to the middle of the city and with its grassy slopes capped by a charmingly designed formal park, is isolated and conical and rises to a height of about 250 feet. Brandon Hill, so named from the likeness of its shape to that of the much higher Brandon Hill in Ireland, was once crowned by the small chapel of St. Brendan to which, in the Middle Ages, Irish sailors resorted. The medieval topographer William Worcestre, who describes the chapel, also likens the hill to that of Calvary. The chapel has gone, but there are traces of earthwork fortifications thrown up in the Civil War. The hill is now conspicuously crowned by the Cabot Tower, in a vaguely Venetian Gothic style and started in 1897 to mark the 400th anniversary of John Cabot's landing near the northernmost tip of Newfoundland.

Just in the Woodspring District of Avon County, but for over twenty years now the property of the City of Bristol, the Ashton Court estate is a magnificent open space, available for many types of recreation and centred on its historic mansion of various dates (see pages 14 and 58). Ashton Court's scenery includes open tableland, a deer park and grassy slopes from which, as in this view, one gets various views back into parts of the city. The Park is the taking off point for hot air balloons participating in the races or festivals which have made Bristol the country's leading centre for this particular pursuit.

On the Downs.

Brandon Hill and the Cabot Tower.

Right Snuff Mills park in the Frome valley, Stapleton.

Ashton Court, with part of Bedminster beyond; the venue for the annual balloon fiesta.

Part of Castle Park, with the ruins of St. Peter's Church.

The Avon Gorge and the Suspension Bridge: Dundry in the distance.

Looking along Welsh Back, newly landscaped and planted.

Cumberland Basin Lock:
dockworkers' cottages, 1831.

New life in Bathurst Basin.

INNER WATERWAYS

The two arms of Bristol's river harbour pierce the very middle of the city. Since 1809, when the tide was shut out by the completion of the Floating Harbour, the water level has been constant, giving Bristol a scenic feature unique in any great English city. Till recent years Bristol's Floating Harbour was a busy port for cargo ships of small or medium size. But apart from sand dredgers its commercial use has now ended, and the largest ships now seen there are visiting warships or other vessels on courtesy calls. It has, however, become an important mooring place for yachts and other pleasure craft, and dinghy sailing takes place to enliven its fine expanse of sheltered water. The Floating Harbour is also the venue of the International Power Boat Festival, an event which brings thousands of visitors to Bristol. Its transit sheds and quayside reaches are finding new uses, as in the late Victorian warehouse occupied by the Watershed Project, for newly built housing and as attractive waterside promenades.

Right From Prince Street bridge: the Floating Harbour, with Redcliffe Parade and St. Mary Redcliffe.

Maritime restoration: S.S. Great Britain (a second mast has now been erected).

Left The Bush Warehouse (1832–37): once serving the tea trade, now the Arnolfini Arts Centre.

Floating Harbour: a nautical scene.

Visiting minesweepers on Narrow Quay.

Watershed Communications Centre: the covered walk.

THE MODERN PORT

The Port of Bristol's commercial activity, with large cargo ships and tankers often coming in for loading and unloading, is now all in the down-river docks of Avonmouth, Portishead and, closer still to Avonmouth and linked to it by the M.4 Motorway bridge over the Avon, in the great unimpeded expanse of Royal Portbury Dock which Her Majesty the Queen formally opened in 1977. Even the coasters and short-sea traders which still use the port now come to Avonmouth and Portishead, having abandoned the tortuous river channel which winds through the Clifton Gorge and round the horseshoe bend which, despite ample depth at high water, imposes a severe length restriction on ships using the historic City Docks. So it is to Avonmouth, to Portishead where the dock was finished in 1879 and to Royal Portbury that one looks for the varied and colourful bustle of a present-day port, with ship-repairing carried on at Avonmouth. Though Portishead and Portbury are not within the city boundaries, the Corporation of Bristol owns them, along with Avonmouth and the City Docks, as the varied elements in one of Britain's few municipal ports.

The original deep-water dock at Avonmouth was finished in 1877, the Royal Edward Dock extension was opened in 1908, and the eastern arm and the oil basin date from the period between the wars. Most ships which come to the Port of Bristol use Avonmouth Dock, and a wide variety of cargoes, mostly by way of imports, is handled there.

Royal Portbury Dock, still without all the quayside equipment planned for it, has yet to prove itself as a commercial proposition. But there is no doubt about the great feat of modern technology whereby a dock area of some seventy acres, approached by the largest lock in the country, was created out of the estuary flatlands between Avonmouth and Portishead.

Timber being unloaded at Avonmouth.

At Avonmouth: entrance lock,
home from South America.

SHIP REPAIRERS

In Royal Portbury Dock: three visiting ships.

Cumberland Basin Lock: a sand dredger moves out into the tidal Avon.

COMMERCE AND INDUSTRY

Bristol owes much of its importance, and its position as the core of an urban area of well over half a million people, to its having long been the scene both of port and commercial activity and of widely varied industry. In the eighteenth century its combination of commerce and manufacturing made it England's second largest town, and the wide variety of its industry has often shielded it from the worst of unemployment.

Though shipborne trade and warehousing no longer feature in the historic centre north of Bristol Bridge this part of Bristol is still, like a small-scale City of London, of note for the offices of banks, finance houses and building societies, for the Bristol Stock Exchange behind its Edwardian Corinthian columns and for the offices of insurance companies. The move to the city of much of these companies' head office work that was previously done in London has made Bristol one of the country's leading centres of insurance activity. Four companies have already made this move. All in all about nine thousand people find employment in insurance in various buildings in the city. Bristol is certainly, with many solicitors', accountants' and architects' offices as well as those more directly concerned with finance, the business capital of a large section of England. Corn Street and Broad Street, with their important banks, finance houses and offices providing insurance services, notably illustrate a long standing historic truth.

Although Bristol has recently seen a shift, in those employed in the city, from 'production' to 'service' trades the city still contains much industry. This occurs, moreover, in many and varied trades, so that Bristol is not, and never has been, a 'one industry' city. Variety has long distinguished it, acting as a cushion against really serious unemployment should any one industry fall on evil times.

Some ancient, historic industries, such as the production of glass, pottery and soap no longer figure among Bristol's trades. The building of small or medium-sized ships no longer occurs in the Floating Harbour, but ship-repairing is still done at Avonmouth and the building of boats and other small craft is again seen on the site of Hill's Albion Dockyard.

But the activities of British Aerospace, varied engineering and the production and packaging of consumer goods are now the giants among Bristol's industry. At Filton and Patchway, just outside the city boundary, the factories of British Aerospace and of Rolls Royce are still busy and give work to thousands, while at Hartcliffe, on Bristol's southernmost outskirts, the Wills factory, with its office block poised above a small artificial lake and set amid pleasant landscaping, is Europe's largest tobacco factory. Paper and packaging, particularly with the use of cellophane sheeting, is another large Bristol industry; so too are the making of stationery and a wide range of printing. Chocolate and brewing are among the local 'consumer' trades. Plastics, chemicals and paint are all represented, so too are footwear, the making of foundation garments and furniture, joinery and the construction of shop fittings. All these are among Bristol's more traditional industries; more recently, and in keeping with the ability of so pleasant a city to attract newcomers with high technical and professional skill, is a concentration of high-technology firms, in some cases more on research and development work than on the actual production of such goods as silicon chips. These firms have greatly gained from their links with the Universities of Bristol and Bath and with the Bristol Polytechnic.

Insurance in Bristol: a view of the Sun Life offices .

Inside the National Westminster (originally Stuckey's) Bank, by R. S. Pope, 1852.

A view in Corn Street, still, as traditionally, the area of banking and finance.

In Broad Street, Everard's façade, Arts and Crafts polychrome, finished 1902.

Merchants' Hall, the Promenade, the arms of the Society of Merchant Venturers.

Broad Quay House, a terracotta plaque by Philippa Threlfall.

Above, centre Bristol & West annexe: the 'golden ship' weathervane.

Merchant Street, Lloyd's Bank (originally Merchant Tailors' Almshouses, 1701), the Company's arms.

Above Tailors' Court (off Broad Street): heraldic door hood, perhaps c. 1700.

Below The Bristol Stock Exchange, Edwardian classical, City arms in pediment.

Left Christchurch, City; quarterjacks, c. 1740.

The new shot tower rises above the Floating Harbour.

Left Modern offices: the Central Electricity Generating Board, Bedminster Down, and the Bristol United Press Building, Temple Way.

Modern industry: inside the Wills tobacco factory, Hartcliffe, and the Aircraft Assembly Hall, Filton.

Broad Quay: the Bristol & West Building Society offices.

STREETSCAPE

The streetscape of Bristol, and the layout of some of its older areas, reflect the length and variety of the city's history. In the ancient centre, for instance, the alleyway which ran just inside the fortified wall of the early medieval town survives, in continuous stretches, in streets and alleys which still run from High Street, via St. Nicholas Street, Leonard Lane and Tower Lane, to the far end of Wine Street. Bristol's abruptly hilly nature adds much to the picturesqueness of some sections of the town. Many details add to the charm of a city which combines a rich historic legacy with its continued story of commercial importance.

In the most historic part of Bristol the pedestrianised top section of Corn Street is dominated by the Georgian tower and cupola of All Saints' Church; below it a projecting building, of the eighteenth century and jutting beyond the building line of the Exchange, continues the business of a historic coffee house going back to Queen Anne's reign. The 'Nails', bronze pillars of the seventeenth century on which cash deals were once conducted by those who 'paid on the nail', are among England's most rare and famous pieces of street furniture.

Between Small Street and Broad Street the attractive enclave of Albion Chambers was created, in its present form, by the widening out of the earlier alley of Small Street Court. The work was done about 1835 by John Langley and the Chambers, above older cellars, were Bristol's first purpose-built office or professional accommodation. Albion Chambers were at first entered only from Small Street, but the passageway into Broad Street, giving lawyers better access to the courts in the new Guildhall, was cut through in 1844.

One of central Bristol's outstanding attractions is the Broad Street façade, with its brilliant decoration of coloured tiles, of what was once the works of Edward Everard the fine art printer. Finished in 1902, it is England's most spectacular façade of its kind. The decorative work, including figures of Gutenberg and William Morris with their founts of type and also displaying a winged figure symbolising literature and another holding symbols of truth and enlightenment, was by W. J. Neatby, then head of Doulton's department of ceramic decoration. Some of the façade's flower and tree motifs also occur in Neatby's work in the Royal Arcade at Norwich.

A landscaped park has been created in the city centre, filling most of the bomb-devastated area between High Street and the far end of Castle Street. A historic feature is the ruined fabric of the Norman and early Perpendicular St. Peter's Church, preserved by the city as a historic ruin and perhaps the oldest of Bristol's many ancient churches.

King Street, one of Bristol's best for historic architecture, was created in two phases. First, from about 1650, came the houses on its northern side; a survivor of those gabled buildings is seen behind the traffic sign. The southern side, whose best known feature is the gabled range which includes the Llandoger Trow inn, is of 1664; the street so created was named after King Charles II. On the right the varied buildings include the low gabled range (of 1652–56) of St. Nicholas' Almshouses, the imposing Coopers' Hall of the 1740s, the modern front of the Theatre Royal complex, Edwardian and Victorian warehouses now used as offices and, in the far distance, the Georgian blocks of the old City Library. The eastern end of this street has now become an attractive pedestrian area.

One of Bristol's supreme glories, and England's finest equestrian statue, is the bronze figure of William III in the middle of Queen Square. The king is shown in Roman armour and riding, in the Roman manner, without stirrups. A masterpiece by the immigrant Flemish sculptor Rysbrack it was made in London in 1735–36 and then brought to Bristol. As Rysbrack's biographer has said it is "a statue which England might well be proud of and recommend her visitors to go and see".★

The steep late Georgian shopping street of Park Street has been repaired by the filling in of many gaps caused by wartime bombing. Its top end is dominated by the great Gothic tower of the Wills Memorial Building of the University of Bristol. Designed before the First World War by Sir George Oatley the buildings were finished in 1925. Though it is less than sixty years old the tower, one of England's last really successful period buildings, has become a symbol of Bristol and an essential feature in the local scene.

★M. I. Webb, *Rysbrack,* 1954, p. 140.

In Corn Street: the pedestrianised top section, with All Saints' Church, the Georgian Coffee House, two of the four 'Nails', and part of the Exchange.

TELEPHONE
16

Market miscellany: Marco's steps, up from Baldwin Street; the Market, and the back of the Exchange; Victoria fountain in St. Nicholas Street.

Left A quiet office precinct: Albion Chambers, started c. 1835.

Christmas Steps, and restored houses in Colston Street.

The urban scene: Park Street and the University tower; Queen Square, the statue of William III, by Rysbrack; King Street, looking west.

Orchard Street:
early Georgian, whitewash over brick.

Right Picturesque townscape in St. Michael's Hill.

HISTORIC BUILDINGS

A city like Bristol is likely to be rich in the number and variety of its historic buildings. Despite many losses, some deliberate, some accidental as in the bombing of the last war, but some coming from the change, and the desire to improve, which one always finds in any city with a long story of progress and prosperity, Bristol's sheer quantity of historic buildings puts it – along with such places as Oxford, Cambridge, York and Norwich – among the first half dozen of England's most beautiful provincial cities. The losses least easy to excuse – at a time when preservation and conservation are held to be important and when it is proved, in a city seeking to attract new residents and tourists, that amenity pays – are some of the acts of destruction of the last thirty years. Consolation comes, however, from a much happier story since about 1970, from Bristol's good present record in conservation and from the use of public money for the preservation and renovation of fine buildings down to, and including, the best of those built last century. Of all the great commercial and industrial cities of this country Bristol is the one with the greatest riches, from the Norman period onwards, of historic architecture. The story of its buildings has been set out, with almost definitive authority, in the book by Andor Gomme, Michael Jenner and myself which appeared early in 1979.* Moreover, Tony Aldous† and others have shown that, conservation apart, Bristol has, in the last twenty years, acquired no mean wealth of new modern buildings.

Most of Bristol's medieval architecture appears in its churches. Not much survives from the Elizabethan period or from the seventeenth century. But the Georgian age, and the architects working in the city in the nineteenth century, have left a great and varied wealth of domestic, public and religious buildings. A few of these are illustrated, with short explanations, in this section, in that on churches and in the pages on Clifton.

**Bristol: An Architectural History* by Andor Gomme, Michael Jenner and Bryan Little, 1979.
†*Changing Bristol* by Tony Aldous, 1979.

Theatre Royal (the modern façade) and the Coopers' Hall (present entrance), and the auditorium.

The Exchange, by John Wood the Elder of Bath, finished in 1743.

London
Coffee House
1713

Far Left In Corn Street: Lloyd's (originally Bristol and South Wales) Bank, by Gingell and Lysaght.

Left On Welsh Back: the Granary, from warehouse to 'heavy rock'.

From over the fountain, the Royal West of England Academy.

Kingsweston House, by John Vanbrugh.

Redland Court (now Redland High School), by John Strahan.

Ashton Court, the mansion: various architects and dates, 15th to 19th century.

Far left Dowry Square, Hotwells: Humphry Davy's house.

Left The Lower Arcade, 1824, probably England's finest arcade of its date and type.

College Green: the Council House, by Vincent Harris, started 1935, finished in the 1950s.

The Grammar School, main building, by Foster and Wood.

CHURCHES

Bristol, Norwich and York, of provincial England's historic cities, are the richest in the architecture and furnishings of their old and more modern churches. Norwich, it is true, exceeds Bristol in the number and in the average quality of its medieval places of worship, but has no equivalent of Bristol's fine churches built in a time of eighteenth-century prosperity. York Minster and Norwich Cathedral are greater buildings than Bristol Cathedral, but Bristol's St. Mary Redcliffe is a much finer, more cathedralesque parish church than any parish church in York or Norwich, while the architectural quality of Bristol Cathedral greatly transcends its modest size. Bristol's nineteenth-century churches, of all denominations, were built more modestly than those of some other larger and more thriving provincial cities, but are none the less of great interest, while the city's more recent church building culminated, in 1973, when it saw the opening of Clifton Cathedral, one of England's finest masterpieces of contemporary religious architecture. Bristol's churches take an outstanding place along with the city's other treasures of 'historic' or more recent building design.

The old parts of Bristol Cathedral were once the transepts, the central tower and the choir limb of St. Augustine's abbey of Augustinian canons regular. The fourteenth-century choir, with three alleyways of equal height on the 'hall church' plan, is unique among England's cathedral or abbey churches and makes the building of enormous architectural importance. The nave, modelled on the choir, is Victorian work by G. E. Street.

Originally the church of the Hospital of St. Mark which was founded in the thirteenth century, the Lord Mayor's Chapel had later additions, while its East end, and the fine timber roof of its nave and choir, date from soon after 1500. Its splendid medieval and Renaissance glass, its tombs and mural monuments and other fittings and furnishings make the building an incredibly rich treasure house of various religious arts.

Christ Church, in the very middle of the original town, replaced a medieval building late in the eighteenth century. The beautiful classical church, with its fine steeple and with its saucer-domed interior indebted to that by Gibbs in St. Martin's in the Fields, was by the local architect William Paty. The original altarpiece was reinstated, about fifty years ago, as a screen; the present windows are of the 1880s.

St. Nicholas' Church, now splendidly renovated as a museum of local history and church art, was rebuilt, above a fine vaulted crypt of about 1370, in the Georgian Gothic of the 1760s. The architect was James Bridges, but Thomas Paty supervised its completion in 1769. Its noble plaster ceiling was destroyed by bombing, but the admirable tower and spire, with oval lucarnes recalling an eighteenth-century date, survived.

The Church of St. John the Baptist is one of four built on tactically obsolete stretches of Bristol's Norman town walls. In its present form it is an attractive late fourteenth-century building, above a fine vaulted crypt, in the early Perpendicular style. Its best known feature, and one of Bristol's best loved attractions, is the tower with its spire (once shared with the adjacent Church of St. Lawrence) poised above a vaulted gateway which still has its portcullis groove.

Standing proudly on the little ridge whose exposed rock face gives the area its name, St. Mary Redcliffe is, as Queen Elizabeth I said in 1574, the "finest, goodliest and most famous parish church in England". Originally a twelfth-century chapel of ease in the large parish of Bedminster, it was mostly rebuilt at various times in the fourteenth century. With its doubly aisled transepts, its magnificent stone vaults and its eastern Lady Chapel, it gave the impression of a moderate-sized abbey church or a small cathedral. Much of its tall spire fell down in 1445 and was rebuilt, in the 1870s, to its original height of about 300 feet. Some interesting tombs and brasses, and fine Baroque ironwork, help to make this church a 'must' for all who live in, or visit, Bristol.

The Temple Church, originally founded by the Knights Templar in the twelfth century, but after the 1330s the parish church of the Holy Cross, was gutted by wartime bombing. But the famous leaning tower, of two separate dates in the Perpendicular period and built, like the campanile at Pisa, with inadequate foundations on alluvial soil, survived. The ruins are now cared for by the Department of the Environment.

In 1739 John Wesley built his New Room in the Horsefair as a meeting and worshipping place for his followers at a time when he was denied the use of the parish churches. It did not, at first, rank as the chapel of a separate denomination. It was enlarged and remodelled, with quarters upstairs for itinerant preachers, in 1748. Beautifully renovated some fifty years ago it displays an 'auditory' interior typical of its time and of the churches built after Wren designed many in the City of London. It ranks as the oldest Methodist chapel anywhere, and is a place of pilgrimage for Methodists from all over the world.

Originally a private chapel for the owner of Redland Court, his tenants and servants, Redland Church is a delightful building, combining Palladian and Baroque influences, of 1740–43. The architect was probably John Strahan. Inside one finds excellent carved woodwork, and sculpture by Rysbrack.

Of Bristol's recently built churches the one at Lockleaze, by T. H. B. Burrough and finished in 1956, is octagonal, of concrete slabs and with a projecting sanctuary-cum-Lady Chapel. Its striking belfry is made up of concrete struts. The church has fine glass by Margaret Trehearne and concrete sculpture by Ernest Pascoe.

Another striking modern church is the Catholic one of St. Bernadette, conspicuously sited as one enters Bristol along the Wells Road. Its brick walls, and double hyperbolic paraboloid roof, enclose a square interior arranged diamondwise. It was designed by James Leask, of the local architectural firm of Kenneth Nealon, Tanner and Partners.

The richly coloured main windows in the narthex of Clifton Cathedral are by Henry Haig. They represent Pentecost with its rushing, fiery flames and the more relaxed feeling of Jubilation after one has received the gift of the Holy Spirit.

For more on Bristol's churches, see Bryan Little's two booklets, *Churches in Bristol*, 1978 and *Church Treasures in Bristol*, 1979.

An answer to Pisa: the 15th century leaning tower of Temple (Holy Cross) Church.

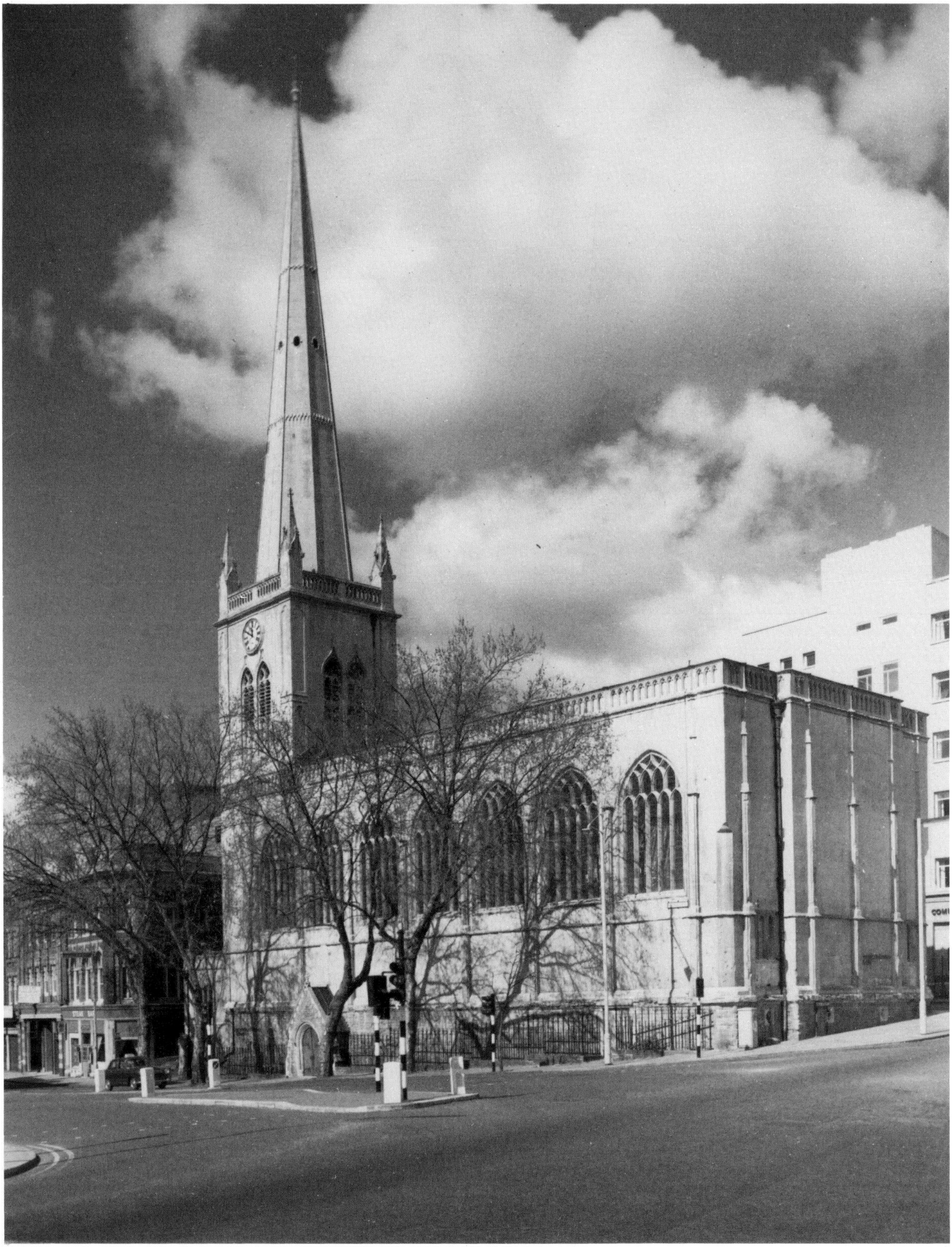

St. Nicholas' Church (now the Museum of Local History and Church Arts), as rebuilt by James Bridges and Thomas Paty in the 1760s.

Right a mid-eighteenth century gem: Redland Church, mainly by Strahan.

THIS WAY TO
THE LIVING
ROOMS →

A civic church: the Lord Mayor's Chapel (originally St. Mark's Hospital) varying dates c. 1230–1500.

Left Methodist shrine: John Wesley's 'New Room' in the Horsefair.

Christ Church, by William Paty, showing the influence of Gibbs.

Two modern churches: Lockleaze, by T. H. Burrough, opened 1956,
and St. Bernadette's (Roman Catholic), Wells Road, by Kenneth Nealon, Tanner and Partners, finished 1968.

Bristol Cathedral: the great gateway of St. Augustine's Abbey, late Norman below, early Tudor above.

Right Bristol Cathedral, from the south-east; mostly 14th and 15th centuries.

Below St. Mary Redcliffe, from the north-west.

Below right Broad Street, the steeple over the gateway: St. John the Baptist's Church, c. 1380.

Above King Street: St. Nicholas' Almshouse, gables and mullions, 1652–56.

Above right King Street: Merchant Venturers' Almshouse (founded for retired seamen), c. 1699.

Right Colston Street: Foster's Almshouse; chapel of the Three Kings of Cologne, c. 1480; the rest, Burgundian late Gothic, 1861, 1880–83, by Foster and Wood.

St. Michael's Hill: Colston's Almshouse, c. 1690.

Almshouses

Bristol has long been well known for the number and picturesqueness of its almshouses. Their foundation started well before the Reformation; some of those built later were, like the bombed Unitarian Almshouse in Stokes Croft, for members of particular religious groups, while bachelordom or spinsterhood were essential in occupants of the early Georgian Ridley's Almshouse. The last of Bristol's almshouses was built as late as the 1890s. Some have been destroyed at various times, while a few were bombed. But some of those still surviving are attractive buildings which add much to the charm of the local scene.

Of those illustrated St. Nicholas' and the Merchant Venturers' (or Seamen's) almshouses stand one at each end of King Street. The gabled and mullioned range of St. Nicholas' parish almshouses was built, on a site once that of the ditch in front of the thirteenth-century town wall, in 1652–56; it has rich plasterwork in what used to be the committee room. Half of the charming open court of the Seamen's Almshouse was destroyed, along with the Merchant Venturers' Hall, by bombing. Its origins are medieval; its date plaque of 1699, seen along with a fine achievement of the Merchant Venturers' arms, refers to the year when its rebuilding was finished.

Foster's Almshouse stands at the top of Christmas Steps. Its chapel of the Three Kings of Cologne is the original of 1484, but the other buildings, a picturesque blend of diapered brickwork, stone dressings, timber and tiles in various colours, is a Burgundian Gothic rebuild, by the Bristol architects Foster and Wood, of various Victorian dates.

Bristol's finest almshouse is Colston's in St. Michael's Hill. Edward Colston founded it in 1690 and its dignified three-sided court, with a chapel in the middle of one side and providing both for men and women, is typical of such buildings put up in the time of Wren. Celia Fiennes, a traveller in the 1690s, said that the new building, which she describes in detail, was "more like a gentleman's house" than an almshouse.

INNS

Bristol has long been well supplied with inns, and their number has reflected the city's position as a seaport, commercial and market town, with more thirsts to be slaked than those of the resident population. Between 1752 and 1764 there were, for instance, over eight hundred inns in Bristol. Even if not all of them were simultaneously in business in any one year the number seems vast for a city whose population was not much above 50,000. Many were in the central or harbour areas which were the haunts of seamen and other visitors. Early in the eighteenth century there had been over two hundred, while Sketchley's Directory of 1775 lists 445. Though there are now fewer pubs per thousand of the population than two centuries ago, Bristol still has many inns, some of them of great charm and character, with buildings of value in Bristol's heritage of historic charm.*

In Frogmore Street the frontage of the Hatchet is a picturesque, half-timbered Jacobean composition; the inn has, in recent years, been given sympathetic extensions, on what is now an island site, at the sides and back.

The Llandoger Trow in King Street, named from the trows, or sailing barges, which once plied up the Wye to Llandogo, was once part of a five-gabled range; two bays of the building were bombed in the war. Its date of 1664, when the second half of the street was laid out, makes it a late example of the timber-framed architecture more normally associated with medieval or Elizabethan builders.

Downstairs in Broad Street the Malt and Hops picturesquely occupies cellars whose masonry details indicate a thirteenth or fourteenth century date.

Though its history goes back hundreds of years the Rummer Tavern's present building is of 1743 when its erection came as part of the reorganisation of the Market area when the Exchange was built.

The most unusual of Bristol's pubs is the floating one at the bottom of St. Augustine's Reach. The 'Lochiel' was built for Macbrayne's at Dumbarton and finished in 1939. Till 1970 this motor vessel of 577 tons plied among the Western Isles. Later she was laid up, but was saved from the shipbreakers by being towed to Bristol to be fitted out as a floating pub.

Another inn, lately fitted out in a renovated building which first served a very different purpose, is the Pump House close to the channel between the Cumberland Basin and the Floating Harbour. The mid-Victorian Italianate building was originally a pump house for the hydraulic machinery which once worked the lock gates.

*See Helena Eason's *Bristol's Historic Inns*.

The half-timbered Llandoger (Llandogo) Trow, a famous landmark in King Street.

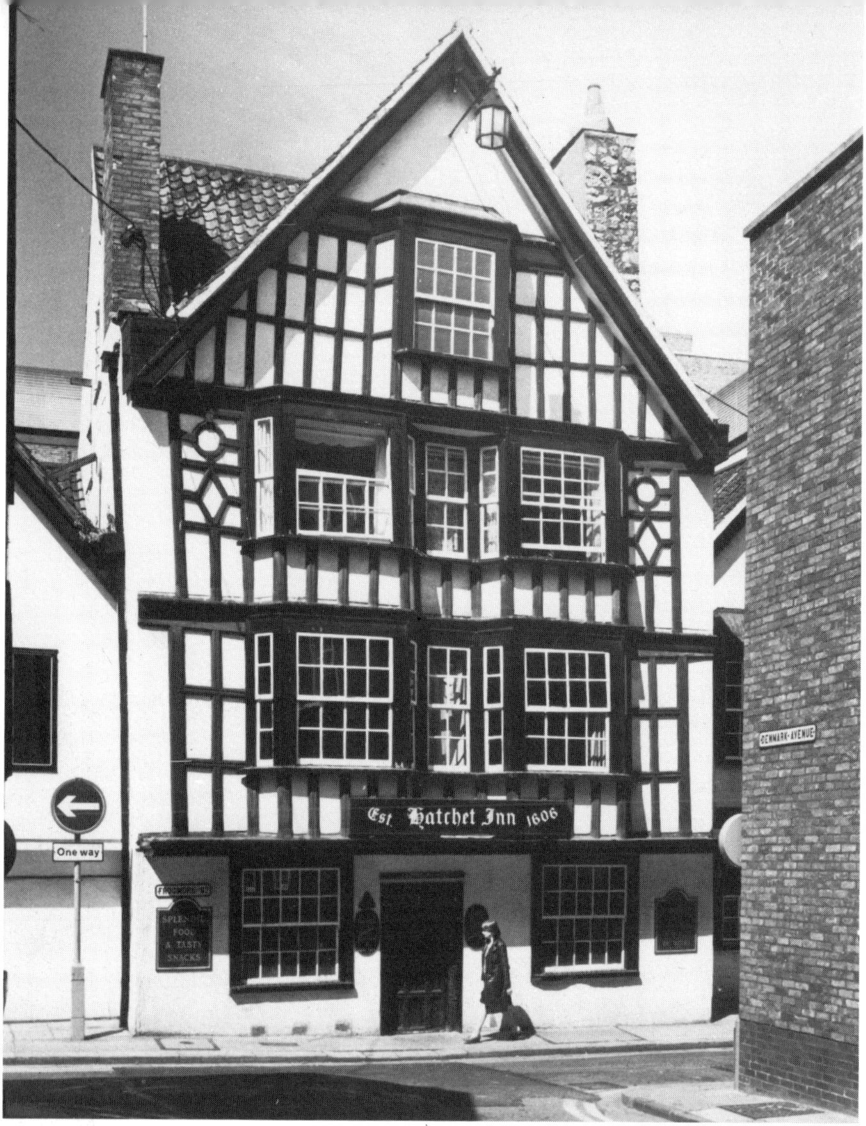

Some more pubs: the Hatchet, half-timbered, c. 1630; the Rummer, as rebuilt c. 1740; the Inn on the Quay (M.V. Lochiel); down in the cellars, partly c. 1300, of the Malt and Hops.

LOCHIEL

THE RUMMER
BUTCHE

Clifton Down: the Observatory,
originally a windmill, seen from the Suspension Bridge.

HOTWELLS AND CLIFTON

Hotwells down by the river and upper Clifton were once both in the same Clifton parish and their history is inter-connected. Hotwells, with warm water coming up through the tidal mud of the Avon, has long ceased to be a spa. Its specifically spa buildings – a Pump Room and two Long Rooms for social gatherings – have long since been destroyed. But the area is still of great charm, with Georgian squares and terraces built to lodge the Hotwell's fashionable visitors. Many fine houses have recently been renovated, and the whole area is the scene of new and more sophisticated residential life. The oldest of the squares in Hotwells is Dowry Square, and the attractive houses along its top end go back to the early Georgian period.

A row of dock workers' cottages, dated 1831 and sited by one of the locks into the Floating Harbour, is another charming feature.

Upper Clifton, or Clifton on the Hill, developed as a late Georgian resort and then as a residential area. With its romantic scenery, its fine architecture of single houses and formal groupings, and its picturesque corners, it has been called England's most beautiful suburb. It is as if an equivalent to Bath or Cheltenham existed here, not as a town on its own but as a part of a large commercial and industrial city. Parts of Clifton have, in recent years, been much transformed and enlivened by an influx of University staff and students and of young professional people and artists. Antique and crafts shops, boutiques and restaurants and wine bars have made Clifton, as it were, the Chelsea of the West of England.

Rising above the great precipice of St. Vincent's Rocks and built within the ramparts of an Iron Age hill fort, the Observatory was originally a windmill tower but was refitted, with its camera obscura which reflects superb views of the rest of Bristol and the beginnings of South Wales, early last century.

Overlooking the Suspension Bridge, the late Georgian houses of Sion Hill are picturesquely varied in their details.

The formal composition at the top end of the beautiful enclosure of the Mall has been much altered to make way for shops. Its dignified central building, once Clifton's Assembly Rooms, is by Francis Greenway who later became the first important architect to work in Australia.

Magnificently sited and the longest crescent in England, Royal York Crescent was started about 1790 but was not finished, with the 'Regency' addition of first-floor balconies, till after the Napoleonic Wars.

The Paragon, another Regency crescent, with its balconies on the convex side and with an unusual row of curved porches, superbly exploits its dramatic position above the top end of the Avon Gorge.

Clifton College was founded in 1862 and has become one of England's best known public schools for boys, with many day pupils as well as boarders. Its buildings, mostly by Charles Hansom but with later extensions and alterations to the chapel, make a fine grouping of the 'educational' late Gothic favoured by the Victorians.

Close to the College the Clifton Zoo was started in 1835. It has always been of interest to botanists as well as to zoologists. It is notable for the splendour of its gardens, for its fine collection of animals and for some striking recent buildings.

An important recent addition to the Clifton scene, and widely accepted as one of England's best examples of modern church architecture, is the Roman Catholic Cathedral of Saints Peter and Paul. Finished in 1973 its plan is that of an elongated hexagon, of concrete and mostly clad with panels of Aberdeen granite chips; its exposed concrete and the pinkish colour of these panels answer to the Bath and pennant stone of the area in which the Cathedral is set. The concrete members of its striking flêche are seen, above trees, as a modern foil to the fine neo-classical range of Worcester Terrace.

The Suspension Bridge, from the Clifton side.

Left Royal York Crescent, the western end.

Right The Paragon, with superb views.

Clifton: across the old churchyard, Birdcage Walk.

On Sion Hill.

Looking down the Mall, Clifton.

Clifton: Roman Catholic Cathedral of s.s. Peter and Paul, opened 1973.

Clifton Cathedral: the Pentecost window, by Henry Haig, and part of another window.

The Red Lodge: the main parlour, late Elizabethan.

Georgian House Museum, Great George Street, c. 1790; the dining room.

CLIFTON
ANTIQUES
MARKET
PM
P.M
GALLERIES
TYNDALL & CO
SOU 287S

ARORA
INDIAN
CRAFTS
DRESSES, GIFTS
CHEMIST
CYCLING
PROHIBITED

Left From Boyce's Avenue to Victoria Square.

Flora and fauna, a view in the Zoo.

Clifton College: mostly by Charles Hansom, started 1862.

Henbury

Going north from Clifton, and through the historic area of Westbury-on-Trym, with its splendid church, its collegiate buildings and its old village centre, one comes to Henbury, once an outlying village in southern Gloucestershire whose recorded history goes back to 692 when land in Henbury was given to the Bishops of Worcester. Henbury has a fine medieval church and its village centre is one of Bristol's more attractive conservation areas.

Henbury's best feature is the Blaise estate, with its deep wooded valley, its classical mansion now used as a Folk Museum and its Georgian Gothic hilltop 'castle'. It is one of Bristol's great glories and a West of England equivalent, at least, to Kenwood in London.

Blaise 'Castle' is near the site of a medieval chapel of St. Blaise from whom the whole estate now gets its name. It is a Georgian Gothic building, by the architect Robert Mylne and finished in 1766: an exactly similar castle, by the same architect and sited on a hill near Shrewsbury, fell down fifty years ago. Mentioned by Jane Austen in *Northanger Abbey,* Blaise Castle was originally roofed and used as a summer residence and, more recently, as a private museum. A few years ago it suffered serious dilapidation, but is now being repaired.

Blaise Hamlet was built by the Harford family who owned the late eighteenth-century Blaise Mansion. The ten cottages were finished in 1811 and were for the most part designed by John Nash. They were planned as retirement homes for old servants of the Harfords. This varied group of tiled or thatched houses is England's best example of a 'rustic romantic' hamlet; it now belongs to the National Trust. It is a particular favourite with foreign visitors and a quiet, endlessly fascinating enclave. If one had to show a visitor to Bristol no more than five or six 'sights' Blaise Hamlet would certainly be among them.

A Gothick fortalice: Blaise 'Castle' by Robert Mylne.

Romantic rusticity: Blaise Hamlet, by Nash and John Repton, finished 1811.

Outside the University, with the City Art Gallery in the background.

Higher Education

Bristol is well known for the range and excellence of its independent schools, and it has a full complement of schools under the Avon County Council. It also has a leading position, much stronger than it was some thirty years ago, as the West of England's chief centre of higher education. Moreover Bristol's University, with its high position, after 'Oxbridge', in the order of preference expressed by intending students, is of more than regional note and has a leading position in the modern city's life and economy.

University College, Bristol, was founded in 1876, on a modest scale and for much of its career was sparsely financed despite help from the Frys, other business families and academic figures. Its first special buildings, still used by the University, were started about 1880. In 1909, with the beginning of a massive flow of benefactions from the Wills family, it obtained its Charter and could then give its own degrees, New, architecturally significant buildings, like later ones designed by Sir George Oatley, were opened in 1910.

Soon after the First World War, when student numbers were still modest by present standards, the University's first great outburst of building work produced such well known landmarks as the Wills Memorial Building, the first part of the Physics Laboratory and, across the Downs, the hall of residence called Wills Hall.

Since 1945 the University has expanded greatly, both in its new buildings and in student numbers. It now has over six thousand undergraduate members and over eight hundred post-graduates; a little over half its undergraduates are in such faculties or schools as science, engineering or medical, dental or veterinary studies. Its modern buildings are of varying architectural merit, with better quality, on the whole, in those built for student accommodation. The University also owns, and creditably preserves, some excellent historic buildings. Among these are houses in St. Michael's Hill, the Georgian mansions of the Royal Fort and Clifton Hill House, and the much altered Goldney House whose splendid garden, with its eighteenth-century ornamental buildings, is occasionally open to visitors and surpasses most college gardens in Oxford or Cambridge.

The Polytechnic is a large, widely varied place of education whose activities, with 4,500 whole-time students, 4,500 on part-time studies and many others on short courses, are dispersed in several buildings. Its main campus, where its administration is carried on and where many of its faculties work, is off Coldharbour Lane between Filton and Frenchay. Work on the wide-spreading modern buildings started early in the 1970s. Most of them, designed by the old City Architects' Department or, in the case of the Charles Darwin Building, by the Department of Education and Science's Laboratories Investigation Unit, are steel-framed with cladding panels of precast concrete faced with a pale grey granite aggregate. But rich brown brickwork appears, behind the main buildings, in the attractive Residential Management Unit known as Felixstowe Court, and in the Octagon which serves as a chapel and for musical and social gatherings. A student village houses some of the comparatively small number of the Polytechnic students who live 'on campus'.

Other Polytechnic Departments are elsewhere in Bristol. Some are still in the one-time Merchant Venturers' Technical College in the middle of the city, while others use accommodation, along with Brunel Technical College, in the barrack-like blocks put up on Ashley Down for the Müller Orphanages. The departments of Design and Fine Art are in new buildings at Bower Ashton, in a beautiful setting on the edge of Ashton Park. Teacher training is done at Redland, while the Humanities Department is in the picturesquely grouped Gothic buildings of the 1850s and by the architects Clarke and Norton, once those of the College of St. Matthias for teacher training.

The University: the Royal Fort (Music and Theology Faculties), by James Bridges.

The University: Clifton Hill House.

Right The Polytechnic: St. Matthias' College, by John Norton, early 1850s (now Humanities Department).

Lower right Hiatt Baker Hall of Residence.

Goldney House gardens: the Gothic tower, and the Grotto.

Edwardian pomp: the City Museum and Art Gallery, by Frank Wills.

MUSEUMS AND ARTEFACTS

Since 1894, when the City took over the Venetian Gothic building once that of the privately run Philosophic Institution and Library Society, its Museum and Art Gallery have added greatly to the value and variety of their collections.

The Art Gallery was opened in 1905. It was the gift of Sir William Henry Wills, later Lord Winterstoke, and its designer Frank Wills was the member of the tobacco family who practised as an architect. Its Edwardian Baroque façade imposingly overlooks Queen's Road and stands next to the great tower of the University. This building, enlarged at the back half a century ago, houses the main museum and art collections.

As in other cities, Bristol's Museum and Art Gallery have of late been much improved in the display and presentation of their fine collections; their value to Bristol's culture and education has greatly benefitted from so positive and enlightened a policy. Bristol has also, like other cities, housed parts of its collections away from the main museum and gallery. Some of its treasures are well housed in historic buildings which have thus found excellent new uses. Some specialised collections, of much interest, are in buildings other than those of the City Museum and Art Gallery. They already include Harvey's Wine Museum and the Lifeboat Museum, of national and not merely local scope. Brunel's *Great Britain* has its museum aspect, and one hopes for museum exhibits in the restored Temple Meads railway terminus.

The Elizabethan Red Lodge, much altered and rewindowed early in the eighteenth century, but retaining in its upstairs parlour a rich plaster ceiling, an ornate stone fireplace and its original panelling and internal porch, displays furniture and other treasures down to the early years of the eighteenth century.

The Georgian House Museum, in a fine mansion finished about 1790, is furnished in the style of that period and with some earlier Georgian items.

The St. Nicholas Church Museum is a splendid work of conservation and re-use as well as being the country's best museum of its kind. In the European Architectural Heritage Year of 1975 it won one of the few 'outstanding' awards in the Civic Trust's awards scheme. Its exhibits illustrate Bristol's medieval history and various aspects of church art. Our picture shows the great triptych by Hogarth which once stood in the church of St. Mary Redcliffe and, recently installed, the splendid eighteenth-century canopied pulpit from the Unitarian chapel at Shepton Mallet in Somerset.

One of the most modern sheds in the City Docks has now, for three years, been Bristol's Industrial and Transport Museum. The view of the ground floor section shows some of a fine collection of historic vehicles.

A privately run museum, almost certainly unique in England, is Harvey's Wine Museum. Approached through the firm's offices in Denmark Street it extends, through picturesque old cellars under neighbouring houses and streets, almost as far as the Hatchet Inn in Frogmore Street. The exhibition well illustrates all processes in the making, maturing, storage and bottling of wine. There is a wide-ranging collection of wine glasses, many of them rare pieces of the eighteenth century, on display.

Artefacts

The eighteenth century, when Bristol was at the peak of its commercial success and of its relative importance among England's provincial cities, was also the period when it was conspicuous for fine achievements in craftsmanship and in the applied arts. Outstanding among these were the splendid Baroque ironwork of William Edney, the Delftware which had been made in Bristol at least since the 1650s, the porcelain of Richard Champion's factory and the ornamented glassware of the last years of the century. There was also the fine rococo plasterwork of the Bristol school, much of it by Thomas Stocking and also found in Bath, Corsham and elsewhere. Bristol also had many cabinetmakers who made furniture in the successive styles of the Georgian peiod. At the time of the Poll Book in 1774 and of Sketchley's Directory brought out in the following year seventy-five cabinetmakers are mentioned; the lists do not include apprentices, so that Bristol may have had in all, over a hundred workers in this skilled trade.

In St. Stephen's Church: gates of Baroque ironwork (originally in St. Nicholas') by William Edney.

Bureau bookcase, mahogany with satinwood inlay, by John Evans of Broadmead; bought for fifteen guineas in 1787.

Artefacts of the 18th century: Bristol porcelain teapot, made in Richard Champion's factory; tinglazed earthenware bowl, 'The Mother and her Daughter', probably Bristol; glass plate and finger bowl, by Lazarus and Isaac Jacobs.

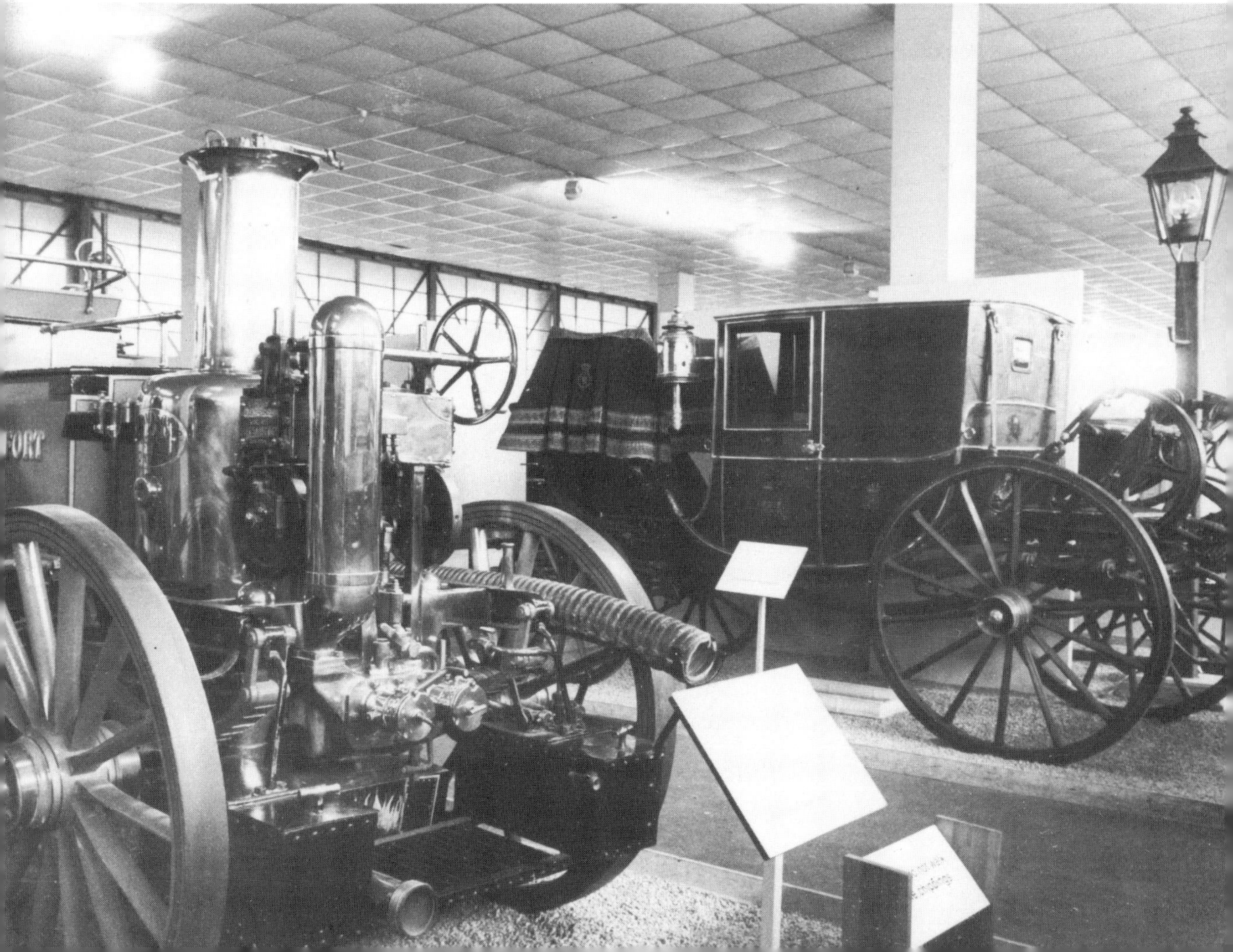

In some Bristol museums: St. Nicholas Church, including Hogarth's altarpiece from St. Mary Redcliffe; Transport and Industrial Museum, on Prince's Wharf.